D0463055

Venus

ELAINE LANDAU

Children's Press®
A Division of Scholastic Inc.
New York   Toronto   London   Auckland   Sydney
Mexico City   New Delhi   Hong Kong
Danbury, Connecticut

Content Consultant

Michelle Yehling

Astronomy Education Consultant

Aurora, Illinois

Reading Consultant

Cecilia Minden-Cupp, PhD

Early Literacy Consultant and Author

Library of Congress Cataloging-in-Publication Data

Landau, Elaine.
Venus / by Elaine Landau.
    p. cm.—(A true book)
Includes bibliographical references and index.
ISBN-13: 978-0-531-12564-9 (lib. bdg.)   978-0-531-14798-6 (pbk.)
ISBN-10: 0-531-12564-5 (lib. bdg.)   0-531-14798-3 (pbk.)
1. Venus (Planet)—Juvenile literature. I. Title. II. Series.
QB621.L36 2008
523.42—dc22   2007004449

All rights reserved. Published in 2008 by Children's Press, an imprint of Scholastic Inc.
Published simultaneously in Canada. Printed in China.
SCHOLASTIC, CHILDREN'S PRESS, A TRUE BOOK, and associated logos are trademarks and/or registered trademarks of Scholastic Inc.
2 3 4 5 6 7 8 9 10 R 17 16 15 14 13 12 11 10 09 08   62

Find the Truth!

Everything you are about to read is true *except* for one of the sentences on this page.

Which one is TRUE?

T or F A spaceship on Venus's surface would crumple like a tin can.

T or F Venus's thick clouds keep the planet's surface cool.

Find the answer in this book.

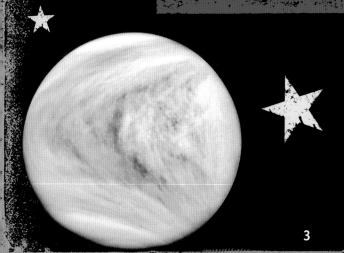

Contents

THE **BIG** TRUTH!

Erupting Venus

Tick volcano

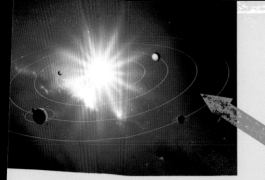

Only Mercury is closer to the sun than Venus is.

Mountain ranges cover parts of Venus's surface.

Venus is often visible from
Earth around the times the
sun rises and sets. Only the
moon shines more brightly
than Venus in the night sky.

Venus

CHAPTER 1

A Trip to Venus

Venus was named after the Roman goddess of love and beauty.

Quick! Name a planet that is bright, hot, and close to Earth. Did you say Venus? If so, you are correct! Venus is sometimes called the evening star. It is the brightest planet that can be seen from Earth.

Venus is the only planet in our solar system that is named after a goddess, not a god.

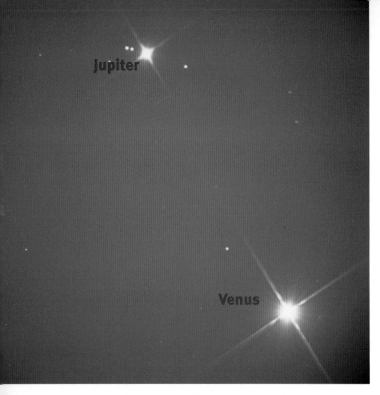

Jupiter

Venus

Venus and Earth are closer together than any other two planets.

Venus is the brightest planet in the night sky. Jupiter is also easy to see at times.

You can often see Venus in the evening sky. You may also be able to see it just before sunrise. People in ancient times used to think Venus was two different objects, a morning star and an evening star. We now know that Venus isn't a star at all. It is a planet.

Venus is Earth's next-door neighbor. If you blasted off in a spaceship today, you might be able to reach Venus in a few months. It could take several years to get to more distant planets, such as Saturn.

Venus is closer to the sun than Earth is. As you flew toward Venus, you would see the sun getting bigger. More of the sun's **radiation** would reach you. This radiation can really heat up objects in space, so your spaceship would need extra protection against the heat.

Venus

Venus passes across the sun, as seen from Earth.

9

Every day is a cloudy day on Venus. The light and dark streaks in this photo are clouds.

It's impossible to see Venus's surface through its clouds.

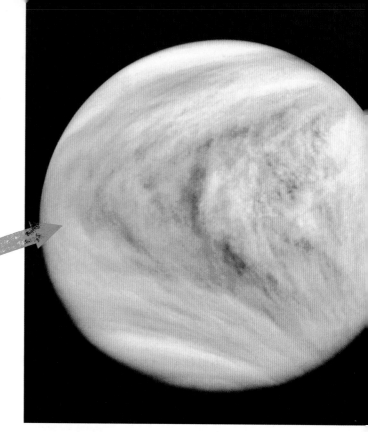

Venus is covered in a thick cloud layer. These clouds trap the sun's heat and keep the planet very hot. Venus collects so much heat that the temperature on its surface gets almost as hot as 864 degrees Fahrenheit (462 degrees Celsius). That's more than twice as much heat as you need to bake a cake!

Discovering Venus

During ancient times, people were interested in the sky. One of these groups of people was the ancient Maya, who lived in what is now Central America. More than 2,000 years ago, they created a calendar based on Venus's movement in the sky. They called Venus the morning star.

The Maya also believed that the sun and Venus were twins. This was because they rose and set in the sky together.

Ancient Mayan priests used drawings such as this to explain the movements of objects in the sky. This is a fragment of a Mayan book.

This artwork shows the sun shining in the sky behind Venus.

Venus in the Solar System

 On Venus, the sun rises in the west.

Venus is Earth's closest planetary neighbor. It is also the second-closest planet to the sun in our **solar system**. The sun and all the objects that **orbit**, or travel around it, make up our solar system. The other planets that orbit the sun are Mercury, Earth, Mars, Jupiter, Saturn, Uranus, and Neptune.

Most of the planets have at least one moon. Combined, they have at least 162 moons! Jupiter has at least 63. Venus has no moon at all.

Venus and Mercury are the only two moonless planets.

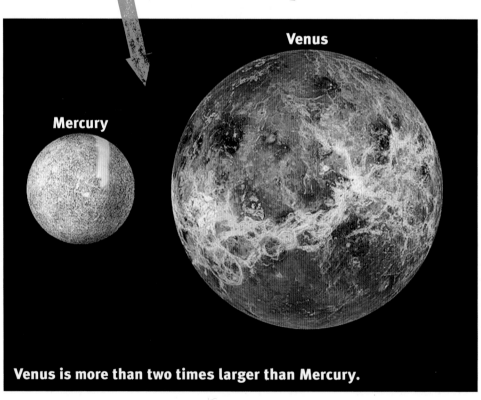

Mercury

Venus

Venus is more than two times larger than Mercury.

The solar system also has **asteroids,** or large chunks of rock that travel through space. It has hundreds of **comets,** or chunks of ice and dust that orbit far from the sun. Pluto also orbits the sun. **Astronomers** used to think Pluto was a planet. Astronomers are scientists who study planets and other objects in space. Now they call Pluto a **dwarf planet**. There are at least two other dwarf planets besides Pluto in the solar system.

Venus's Solar System

Pluto (dwarf planet)

Uranus

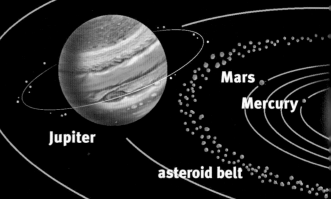
Jupiter

Mars

Mercury

asteroid belt

Venus

- Second planet from the sun
- Sixth-largest planet
- Diameter: 7,521 mi.
  (12,104 km)
- One day equals 243 Earth days
- One year equals 225 Earth days

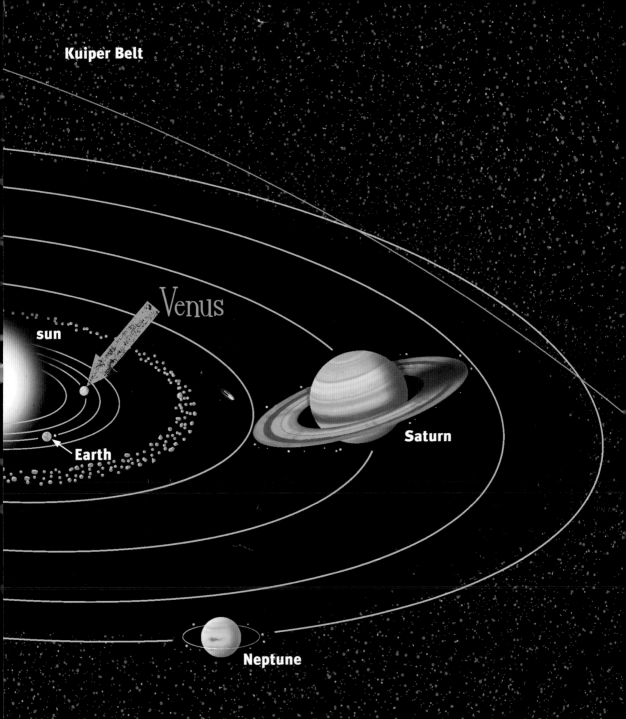

Kuiper Belt

sun

Venus

Earth

Saturn

Neptune

Venus on the Move

Every planet has to travel a different distance to orbit the sun. Venus is close to the sun, so it doesn't have to travel as far as most planets to complete one orbit.

Each planet also orbits at a different speed. Venus orbits very quickly. It moves faster than Earth does.

Venus orbits the sun at about 78,000 miles per hour!

This image shows the four planets closest to the sun. The line through each planet is its orbit. The lines around planets show the orbits of their moons.

Gravity brings this skydiver back down to Earth.

The time it takes a planet to orbit the sun is one year on that planet. It takes Earth 365 days to orbit the sun. Venus takes 225 Earth days to orbit once. This means a year on Venus equals 225 Earth days.

How does Venus stay in its orbit around the sun? Like all of the planets in our solar system, Venus stays in its orbit because of a force called **gravity**. Gravity pulls objects toward each other. The sun's gravity tugs on all the planets. It keeps the planets orbiting, rather than floating off into space.

A Sluggish Spinner

As the planets orbit the sun, they rotate, or spin, on an axis. An axis is an imaginary line that runs from north to south through the center of a planet. Each planet takes a different amount of time to rotate on its axis. The time it takes a planet to spin around once on its axis equals one day on that planet. As it spins, the side facing the sun has daylight. The side facing away from the sun is dark.

Venus is an extremely slow spinner. This means a day on Venus is 243 Earth days long. A day on Venus is 18 Earth days longer than a year on Venus.

Venus spins in the opposite direction from the direction Earth spins. The sun rises in the west and sets in the east on Venus. On Earth, it's just the opposite!

A day on Venus is longer than a year on Venus!

Venus's Rotation

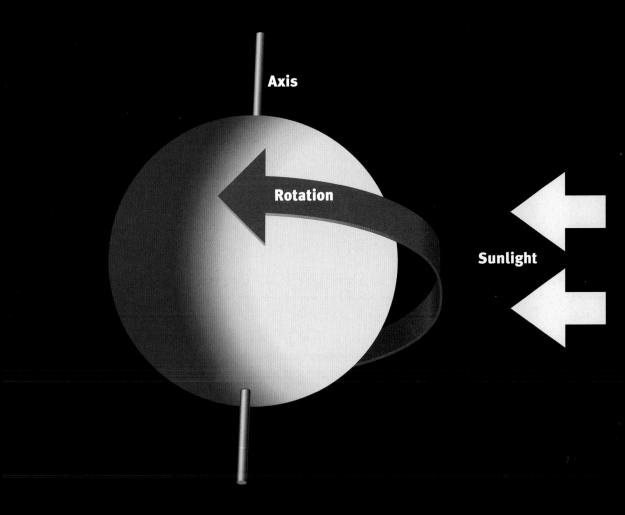

Axis

Rotation

Sunlight

The red arrow in this diagram shows the direction of Venus's rotation. Venus rotates in the opposite direction from most of the other planets. It is daytime on the side that faces the sun. As the planet rotates, new parts move into the sunlight.

This image of one of Venus's large volcanoes was created on a computer. Many of Venus's surface features were created by volcanoes and their flows of lava. Lava is hot melted rock or melted rock that has cooled and hardened.

CHAPTER 3

Venus Is NOT Like Earth

Venus has more volcanoes than any other planet.

Venus has sometimes been called Earth's twin. In many ways, Venus and Earth are alike. The two planets are about the same size. They are both made of rock and metal. In many other ways, however, Venus is very different from Earth. A visit to Venus would be a *really* hard trip.

There is a dried-up riverbed on Venus that is longer than any river on Earth.

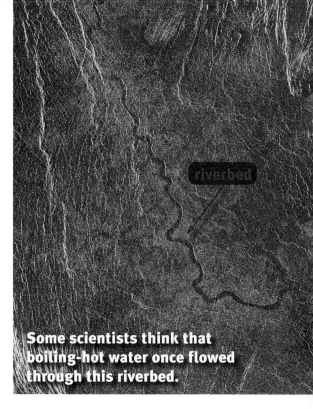

riverbed

Some scientists think that boiling-hot water once flowed through this riverbed.

One big problem for humans on Venus would be the heat. No human being could survive Venus's extremely high temperatures. The temperature is so high that there is no liquid water on the planet. Any water would be likely to boil away! Even if people could take the heat, they would die of thirst.

Heat and thirst would not be your only problems. You would not be able to breathe on Venus. There is no oxygen—only toxic gases.

Too Much Pressure!

Imagine that you found a way to survive Venus's heat and toxic gases. Here's another problem. The pressure of Venus's **atmosphere** would crush you. An atmosphere is the blanket of gases that surrounds a planet or a moon. Every planet's atmosphere creates pressure. You don't notice Earth's atmospheric pressure pushing on your body. The pressure on Venus is much stronger than it is on Earth. Venus's pressure is strong enough to crush a spacecraft like a tin can!

This artwork shows Venus's surface.

CHAPTER 4

One Hot Planet

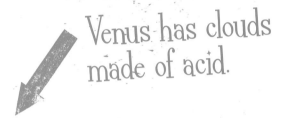

Venus has clouds
made of acid.

The average temperature on Venus is about 854°F (457°C). That's hot enough to melt a lead cannonball. Venus is even hotter than Mercury—the planet closest to the sun! What makes Venus so hot?

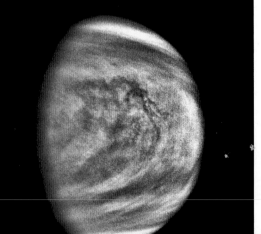

The thick clouds above Venus trap the sun's heat. The clouds rain burning acid onto the planet's surface.

Greenhouses hold the sun's warmth so plants can grow, even in winter. Venus's atmosphere works like a greenhouse to heat the planet.

Venus has a heavy atmosphere all around it. The atmosphere is made mostly of a gas called carbon dioxide.

Carbon dioxide is called a greenhouse gas. In a greenhouse, the sun's warming rays go through the glass. The glass holds heat inside the building and makes it very warm. Plants can grow inside even when it's cold outside.

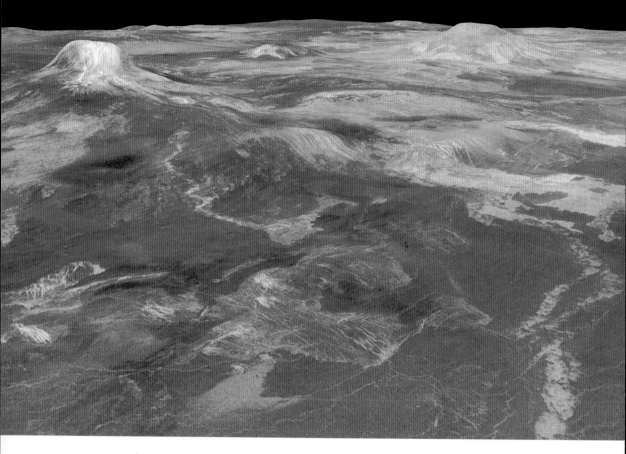

There is no life on the hot, dry surface of Venus.

Carbon dioxide does the same job as the glass in a greenhouse. It traps heat and keeps it close to a planet's surface. Venus's thick clouds keep heat and gases trapped. The heat and gases build up more and more. All that makes Venus a hot planet.

Earth also has carbon dioxide and other greenhouse gases in its atmosphere. Without carbon dioxide, Earth would be too cold for life to survive. Now, scientists are concerned that people are adding too much greenhouse gas to Earth's atmosphere. Carbon dioxide streams into the atmosphere when people burn oil, gasoline, or coal. Extra carbon dioxide can cause Earth to heat up. This is called global warming.

Scientists are very interested in studying the temperature and atmosphere on Venus. Our neighbor planet can show us what happens when the amount of greenhouse gases is very large.

Shield

Shield volcanoes have gentle slopes. Lava erupts from the middle of the volcano. It can flow long distances in all directions. Venus has about 150 large shield volcanoes and about 100,000 smaller ones. Small shield volcanoes are less than 12 miles (19 kilometers) across.

Dome

Dome volcanoes are low, bowl-shaped bumps on the planet. They happen when hot, melted rock pushes out the surface.

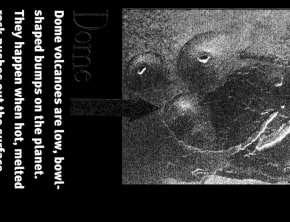

Erupting Venus

Most of Venus is covered in hardened lava. This lava spilled from volcanoes long ago. Three kinds of volcanoes made all this lava. Take a look at them below. Dome and shield volcanoes are seen on Earth as well!

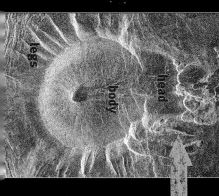

legs

head

body

Tick

This volcano looks like an insect known as a tick. The round "body" is the main part of the volcano. The dark spot is a hole where lava came out. Pits where the ground has sunk in are the "head." Scientists don't know how the "legs" formed.

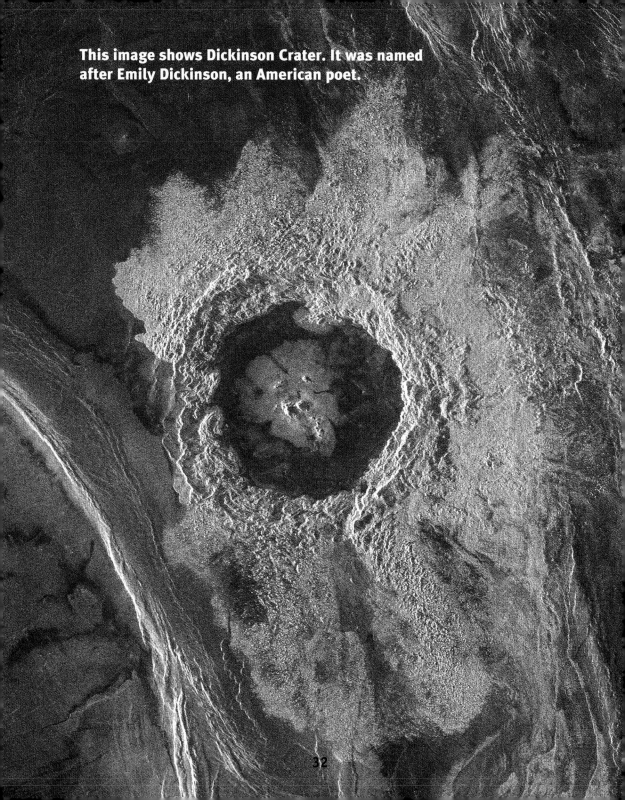

This image shows Dickinson Crater. It was named after Emily Dickinson, an American poet.

CHAPTER 5

On the Surface

 Many of the surface features on Venus have been named after famous women.

Venus is different from Earth in many ways. Being on Venus has been compared to being in a pizza oven. Yet this "oven" has several surface features similar to Earth's. Venus has mountains, **canyons**, and volcanoes.

This photograph shows a caldera, or collapsed volcano, on Venus. The caldera is named Sacajawea after a Native American woman who guided explorers across the United States.

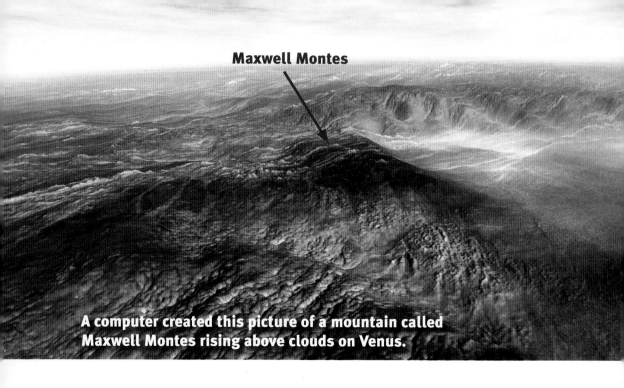

Maxwell Montes

A computer created this picture of a mountain called Maxwell Montes rising above clouds on Venus.

Venus also has clouds hanging above its hot surface. Beneath these clouds, Venus has a rugged surface.

Mountains cover about one-third of the planet. The tallest mountain on Venus is higher than Mount Everest. Mount Everest is the highest peak on Earth. It is about 5 miles (8 km) high. The highest peak on Venus is called Maxwell Montes. It rises 7 miles (11 km) high.

In other areas, Venus has deep canyons. The deepest is 9,500 feet (2,900 meters). Earth's Grand Canyon is only about 5,200 feet (1,585 m) deep.

Thousands of volcanoes cover the planet, too. The largest is Maat Mons. It rises 25,000 feet (7,620 m) high.

Venus also has holes called craters. These craters were formed when asteroids or other objects hit the planet. Venus is not as heavily covered with craters as other bodies, such as Earth's moon. Venus doesn't have a lot of craters partly because of its thick atmosphere. Objects flying through the thick atmosphere become very hot. Most asteroids or **meteoroids** that enter its atmosphere burn up before hitting the surface. Only large space rocks make it to the surface.

Scientists have counted more than 1,600 major volcanoes on Venus. Maat Mons, shown here, is the tallest one.

There is another reason why Venus has fewer craters than other planets or moons. Many craters on Venus were covered over by melted rock. This hot rock oozed out of the inside of the planet. The new rock covered most of Venus's surface. Scientists think that this happened hundreds of millions of years ago.

No Moon for Venus

No one knows why Venus has no moon. Scientists do have an idea how moons formed on other planets, however. Scientists believe that Earth's moon was formed when the planet was young. A planet-sized object rammed into Earth. Huge amounts of rock and other material were flung out into space. Over time, this material clumped together to make our moon.

Why didn't the same thing happen to Venus? It is possible that it did, but the moon drifted off into space. No one knows whether Venus once had moonlight of its own.

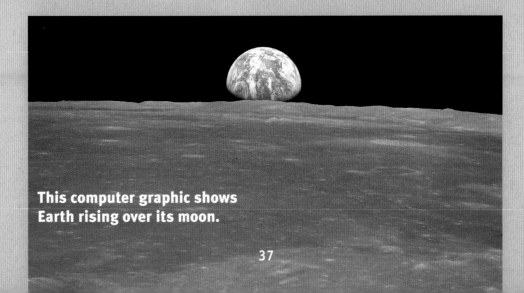

This computer graphic shows Earth rising over its moon.

This artwork shows *Pioneer 13* dropping four probes toward Venus. The probes took measurements of the planet's atmosphere before crash-landing on the surface.

CHAPTER ⭐ 6

Missions to Venus

← The *Pioneer 12* and *13* space probes burned up in Venus's atmosphere.

Astronomers have been interested in knowing about Venus for a long time. It was the first planet studied by an unmanned spacecraft. In the 1960s and 1970s, both the **Soviet Union** and the United States sent spacecraft to Venus. These spacecraft took thousands of photos and gathered information about the planet and its atmosphere.

39

Magellan and More

There have been many other missions to Venus. The *Magellan* spacecraft blasted off on May 4, 1989. It reached Venus in August 1990. From high above the planet, it

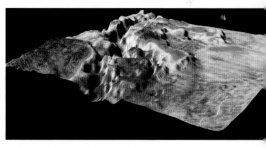

This computer graphic shows some of Venus's hills. It was made from information gathered by *Magellan*.

mapped Venus a little at a time. Astronomers put the pieces together and made a map of almost the entire surface of the planet.

Missions to Venus Timeline

1970
Venera 7
First to land on surface

1961
Venera 1
First craft to study Venus

Mariner 2

1962
Mariner 2
Finds carbon dioxide in atmosphere

All of these missions helped astronomers learn more about Venus's atmosphere and soil. Astronomers also got some close-up photos of the planet's surface.

Other space probes are still out there. In November 2005, *Venus Express* was launched. It arrived near the planet in April 2006. It will loop around Venus's north and south **poles** to map the planet and send back pictures. *Venus Express* is giving astronomers a clearer view of the planet's landscape.

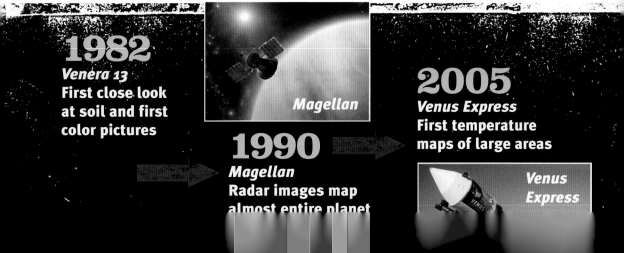

1982
Venera 13
First close look at soil and first color pictures

Magellan

1990
Magellan
Radar images map almost entire planet

2005
Venus Express
First temperature maps of large areas

Venus Express

This artwork shows *Venus Express* approaching Venus. The spacecraft has been orbiting the planet since 2006.

Still other missions are planned for Venus. In 2013 and 2020, space probes to Venus may study its atmosphere more carefully. Spacecraft may even land on Venus and examine samples of its surface! Scientists still have a lot to learn about the closest planet to Earth. It is always good to get to know your neighbors! ★

True Statistics

Year discovered: Unknown

Size: Nearly identical to Earth

Number of moons: 0

Atmosphere: Yes

Surface temperature: About 864°F (462°C)

Distance from the sun: About 67 million mi. (108 million km)

Distance from Earth: About 26 million mi. (42 million km) at its closest point

Length of a day: 243 Earth days

Length of a year: 225 Earth days

Did you find the truth?

T A spaceship on Venus's surface would crumple like a tin can.

F Venus's thick clouds keep the planet's surface cool.

Resources

Books

Alberti, Theresa Jarosz. *Out and About at the Planetarium*. Minneapolis: Picture Window Books, 2004.

Chrismer, Melanie. *Venus*. Danbury, CT: Children's Press, 2008.

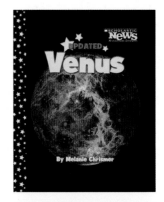

Farndon, John. *Rockets and Other Spacecraft*. Danbury, CT: Franklin Watts, 2003.

Jackson, Ellen. *The Worlds Around Us: A Space Voyage*. Minneapolis: Millbrook Press, 2006.

Kerrod, Robin. *Space Probes*. Milwaukee: World Almanac Library, 2004.

Lassieur, Allison. *Astronauts*. Danbury, CT: Children's Press, 2000.

Prinja, Raman K. *Stars and Constellations*. Chicago: Heinemann Library, 2003.

Richardson, Adele. *Telescopes*. Mankato, MN: Capstone Press, 2004.

Sparrow, Giles. *Asteroids, Comets and Meteors*. Chicago: Heinemann Library, 2002.

Tocci, Salvatore. *Space Experiments*. Danbury, CT: Children's Press, 2002.

Vogt, Gregory. *Comets*. Mankato, MN: Bridgestone Books, 2002.

Organizations and Web Sites

Astronomy for Kids: Venus

www.kidsastronomy.com/venus.htm
Go here for interesting information on Venus and the other planets.

National Space Society

1620 I Street, Suite 615
Washington, DC 20006
202-429-1600
This organization is committed to helping humans live and work in space.

NASA Space Place

spaceplace.nasa.gov/en/kids
Check out this Web site to learn about astronomy in a fun, hands-on way.

Places to Visit

Kennedy Space Center

Kennedy Space Center
FL 32899
www.ksc.nasa.gov
Explore NASA's launch headquarters and learn more about some of the organization's space missions

Smithsonian National Air and Space Museum

Independence Avenue at
4th Street, SW
Washington, D.C. 20560
202-633-1000
www.nasm.si.edu

Important Words

asteroids (AS-tuh-roidz) – large pieces of rock that orbit the sun

astonomers (uh-STRAW-nuh-murz) – scientists who study the planets, stars, and space

atmosphere (AT-mu-sfihr) – the blanket of gases that surrounds a planet or other object

canyons – deep, narrow valleys with steep sides

comets – large chunks of rock and ice that travel around the sun

dwarf planet – a body in the solar system that orbits the sun, has a constant (nearly round) shape, is not a moon, and has an orbit that overlaps with the orbits of other bodies

gravity – a force that pulls two objects together

meteoroids (MEE-tee-uh-roidz) – small chunks of rock, metal, or other debris in space that are up to .6 mile (1 km) in size

orbit – to travel around an object such as a sun or planet

poles – the areas at the very north and very south of a sphere

radiation – waves of energy that flow off of an object

solar system – a sun and all the objects that travel around it

Soviet Union –a country in Eastern Europe and Northern Asia from 1922 to 1991, now broken up into smaller countries

Index

About the Author

Award-winning author Elaine Landau has a bachelor's degree from New York University and a master's degree in library and information science from Pratt Institute.

She has written more than 300 nonfiction books for children and young adults. Although Ms. Landau often writes on science topics, she especially likes writing about planets and space.

She lives in Miami, Florida, with her husband and son. The trio can often be spotted at the Miami Museum of Science and Space Transit Planetarium. You can visit Elaine Landau at her Web site: www.elainelandau.com.

PHOTOGRAPHS © 2008: AP Images: 19 (Dianne Humble), 40 bottom (NASA), 4 top, 41 bottom right; Corbis Images: 11 (Archivo Iconografico, S.A.), 3, 10 (Bettmann), 9 (Mian Khursheed/Reuters), 27 (Joseph Sohm), 7 (Summerfield Press); Getty Images/Digital Vision: back cover; Masterfile/Scott Tysick: 15; NASA: 37 (GRC), 26 (JPL), cover, 4 bottom, 24, 28, 30 left, 30 right, 31, 32, 33, 36 (JPL/Caltech), 14 (Lunar and Planetary Institute), 38 (NSSDC), 40 top (USGS); Pat Rasch: 21 (NASA), 16, 17; Photo Researchers, NY: 22 (David Anderson/NASA), 5 bottom, 34 (David P. Anderson/Southern Methodist Univ./NASA), 25, 41 bottom left (Julian Baum), 42 (Christopher Carreau/ESA), 12 (Mark Garlick), 6 (Gerard Lodriguss), 8 (Rev. Ronald Royer), 5 top, 18 (Detlev van Ravenswaay); Scholastic Library Publishing, Inc.: 44.